WE'VE GOT THIS!

© 2023 Quarto Publishing plc
Text © Rashmi Sirdeshpande 2023
Illustrations © Juliana Eigner 2023

First published in 2023 by words & pictures,
an imprint of The Quarto Group.
1 Triptych Place, London, SE1 9SH, United Kingdom.
T (0)20 7700 6700 F (0)20 7700 8066
www.quarto.com

Assistant Editor: Alice Hobbs
Editor: Kimberley Davis
Designer: Greg Hunt, Banana Bear Books
Art Director: Susi Martin
Associate Publisher: Holly Willsher

A catalogue record for this book is available from
the British Library.

ISBN: 978-0-7112-8492-0

9 8 7 6 5 4 3 2 1

Printed by GPS Group in Bosnia and Herzegovina

MIX
Paper | Supporting
responsible forestry
FSC
www.fsc.org
FSC® C118234

RASHMI SIRDESHPANDE

in partnership with EmpathyLab

WE'VE GOT THIS!

SIX STEPS to build your EMPATHY SUPERPOWER

Illustrated by **JULIANA EIGNER**

words & pictures

CONTENTS

SIX STEPS TO BUILD YOUR EMPATHY SUPERPOWER

"Reading gives you three magical powers: creativity, intelligence and empathy. Empathy is in many ways the most important because it is the one that links you to your community."

CRESSIDA COWELL

FOREWORD

If there's something we need in this world now more than ever, it is empathy.

Without empathy there can be no understanding. It's through stories that we can learn empathy, learn kindness. Stories whether as books, plays or films help us to empathize with the lives and beliefs and histories of ourselves and of others. That way comes understanding.

Everyone is a unique individual - something we should celebrate. When we don't empathize with other people as the individuals they are, we can create stereotypes that aren't true. Stereotypes can lead to misunderstanding people and to conflict. But when we spread empathy, we begin to understand others. It is the same between us and nature. We need to understand and empathize with the environment around us, so we can protect our planet. It is through empathy that we can solve the problems in our world and make it a happier and healthier place for all of us.

Learning at home and school is the best way to encourage empathy. Understanding empathy comes to all of us through our day-to-day life, but most importantly through stories and through the books we read. Stories are the way that most of us first learn about and understand other people. Stories and books can take you all over the world. You can become a sailor, you can become a miner, you can become a mountaineer, you can become anything you want in a book. When you read a story, you live another life in that moment. You go to other places and times, and you meet people you would never normally meet in your daily life. Books really are amazing. If we read as much as we can, and about as many different people as we can, we can find out all about the rest of the world and the wonderful individual people in it. We can spread empathy all around, to people everywhere. If we all do this, I think we can have a much happier and more accepting world.

Books and stories to me are the key to empathy and understanding for everyone. They are the pathway to understanding people as individuals. Read books. Enjoy books. And, most of all, learn from books.

Sir Michael Morpurgo

HOW TO USE THIS BOOK

Empathy is an actual, real superpower that can make a big difference in your life, and in the wider world too. And here's the best bit: we **ALL** have it. But we can **SUPERCHARGE** it. **BOOST** it. That's what we'll do with this book.

It's a six-step process, and we'll go through it together.

STEP 1:
Know what empathy IS.

STEP 2:
Know how empathy WORKS.

STEP 3:
Use your empathy out in the WILD.

STEP 4:
Learn to recognize EMOTIONS.

STEP 5:
Be a BRILLIANT communicator.

STEP 6:
Become the ULTIMATE empathy hero!

Do you know who else is coming on this empathy journey with you? Well, firstly, anyone you can rope in! But **ALSO** this family here. Meet the Sharmas: Shivani and her kids, Isha and Rahul. Just like you, they are well and truly ready to work their empathy muscles and build that empathy **SUPERPOWER!**

Shivani

Rahul

Isha

Yes, empathy is like a **MUSCLE!** The more you use it, the stronger it gets. It's science! We'll get to that soon, as well as lots of other eye-opening, mind-boggling bits, some of which you'll find in boxes like this:

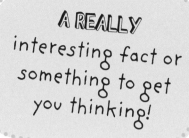

A REALLY interesting fact or something to get you thinking!

You'll also find plenty of activities to help you to understand empathy better, and to give you ideas for how to use it at home, at school and out in the **WILD**.

Finally, you'll spot quotes from some wonderful authors and illustrators dotted about this book because reading is actually one of the most amazing ways you can build up your empathy superpower! More on that very, very soon.

So, that's what we've got in store for you. Let's work through it together, and **POWER UP!**

LET'S GET STARTED...

WE'VE GOT THIS...

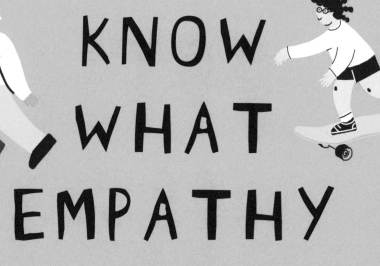

STEP 1:

KNOW WHAT EMPATHY IS

If we're going to build an empathy superpower, we're going to need to wrap our brains around what empathy actually **IS**. So, here we go:

EMPATHY is being able to experience and understand other people's emotions and feelings and their points of view.

Wow, there's a lot in there, isn't there? Let's break it down.

EMOTIONS AND FEELINGS
(we'll talk about these on page 61)

POINTS OF VIEW
how other people see things

The first thing you might notice is that empathy is not about **YOU**. It's about **OTHER PEOPLE**. You're looking outwards, focusing on and caring about someone else. That's very different from just thinking, "Me, me, me!" all the time. Empathy is not about how *you* feel about something, or how *you* see the world. Instead, it's about turning your attention to other people's feelings and points of view.

What do we mean by points of view? **WELL**, two people can see or experience the exact same thing completely differently. In the fairy tale about Little Red Riding Hood, **YOU** might look at Red Riding Hood and think, **"What a sweet little girl,"** but the **WOLF** might think,

"MMM, LUNCH!"

(Or maybe even, "AAAAARRRGH! SCARY HUMAN!")

See? Different points of view!

13

The Sharmas are about to go out. They've got their coats and shoes on, and they're all set, but suddenly it starts **CHUCKING** it down with rain. Isha's jacket has the biggest hood in the whole entire world, so she doesn't really mind. Rahul, the littlest member of the family, is delighted. He can't wait to stomp in puddles and feel the cool rain on his face. Meanwhile, his mum, Shivani, is not so excited. In fact, she's the opposite of excited.

Can you guess why that might be? What if I told you that she **JUST** got her hair done and she has an **EXTREMELY** important meeting today? She might not be too keen to get soaked, right?

Rahul and Shivani are both looking at the same rain pouring down outside, but their feelings about it are so different. From Rahul's point of view, it's a **"YAY!"** moment. From Shivani's, it's a big **"OH NOOOOOOO"**.

When you use your empathy superpower, you can understand another person's point of view **EVEN IF** it's completely different from your own. Yep. It's amazing. Like climbing inside someone else's brain!

OK, let's **PAUSE** for a second.

Empathy doesn't just mean understanding other people's emotions and feelings and their points of view. There was something else in there too. Do you remember what it was? Without peeking?

OK, now you can peek! Did you see it?

Empathy is being able to **EXPERIENCE** and understand other people's emotions and feelings and their points of view. That means that sometimes we feel **WITH** them. It's as if we are **INSIDE** their body and their head, feeling the things they feel.

FEELING WITH CHARACTERS IN BOOKS

Reading books is an incredible way to work that empathy muscle. If you're reading a really gripping and suspenseful book, you might find your heart beating hard when the characters are racing against the clock. BADOOM! BADOOM! BADOOM! You might find yourself turning the pages faster and faster to see what happens and make sure the characters are OK.

Or, if you read a book where the main character feels really sad about something, you might start to feel some sadness in your heart too. And, when something good happens in their life, you'll probably feel really happy for them, just as you would if they were an actual, real friend. Have you ever noticed this?

When this happens, you're feeling *with* the characters. When you read, you step into the characters' worlds, and experience what they experience. **THIS** is **EMPATHY**. You're imagining what it's like to be another person, and you're feeling what they feel.

Books are a kind of **TRAINING GROUND** for getting to know others. Even if you are completely different from a character in every single way imaginable, you can still experience the world the way they do and understand how they feel. That's the power of empathy!

> Your heart is big enough. It really is. And you can always open that heart even wider. Reading helps so much.

"Reading allows us to view the world – and ourselves – through another's eyes and to walk in their shoes for a while, developing understanding. This is the very essence of connecting and communicating effectively with others.

Reading is such a wonderful way to bring people together in a world that increasingly seeks to build walls and barriers between us."

MALORIE BLACKMAN

So, that's what empathy **IS!** Easy, right? Well, **HOLD ON THERE... NOT SO FAST!** There is a little bit more to it than that. You now understand what the word empathy means, but it's also important to know that there are some things out there that might seem like empathy but are actually not quite the same thing. Let's take a look at them now.

EMPATHY IS DIFFERENT FROM SYMPATHY

Imagine you're on the monkey bars with your friend, and they fall down onto the soggy woodchips below. **SYMPATHY** would be shouting down to them, while you hang from the bars above, "Oh no! Poor you! You're all muddy!" **EMPATHY** would be getting down onto the woodchips with them, and seeing things from their point of view.

Sympathy is feeling **FOR** someone. Empathy is feeling **WITH** them.

Sympathy is very "me" and "them" - it keeps us apart. Empathy is connecting with someone. It brings us closer together.

There's something extra-specially lovely about that, isn't there?

EMPATHY IS DIFFERENT FROM RUSHING TO FIX THINGS

You know when someone shares something very personal with you? Maybe that they're feeling down or lonely? Well, you're a good human, right? So maybe the first thing you want to do is try to fix it as fast as you can? To talk about the bright side and make it all better?

That would be like telling your friend who just fell, "Well, look, at least it was only a little fall!" or, "It's lucky you fell down, because it's actually much more fun down there than it is up here on these monkey bars. So that's good... right?"

This desire to help comes from a good place. You don't want someone to be hurt or unhappy, and you want to fix their problems for them. But empathy isn't about immediately jumping in to help or to fix stuff.

When you show empathy, you don't need to say or do anything. You just need to be there for someone else. You can be quiet, or you might say something like, **"I can see you're feeling hurt. I am here for you."** That's enough.

Sometimes, showing that you're there for someone and that you get it — you really do — **sometimes that is the most important thing.** It's about building a connection. Words are powerful, but they aren't always the thing that makes people feel better. Not in the way a deep and genuine connection can. That's empathy for you. See why we call it a superpower?

THE THREE MAIN ELEMENTS OF EMPATHY

1. FEELING: We feel WITH others. This one often happens naturally. When we see someone else feeling something like happiness or anger or sadness, we feel a bit of that emotion too.

2. THINKING: We use our brains and our BRILLIANT imaginations to try to work out how someone else feels and to understand why.

3. ACTING: We are INSPIRED to help others and be kind to them because we have experienced how they are feeling and/or because we really understand them.

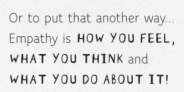

Or to put that another way... Empathy is **HOW YOU FEEL, WHAT YOU THINK** and **WHAT YOU DO ABOUT IT!**

EMPATHY IS DIFFERENT FROM KINDNESS

We use different elements of empathy at different times. Sometimes we **FEEL** a lot with others. Other times, we're **THINKING** about their point of view. And sometimes, while doing that thinking or feeling (or both!), we're inspired to **DO** something to help.

While empathy is not the **SAME** as kindness, it is often the seed of kindness. It grows into kindness. Of course it does. If you feel with someone else and really understand things from their point of view, you'll care about them and feel inspired to be kind to them. Not only that – if they need help with something, the **THINKING** bit of empathy means that you'll have a much better idea of what that something might be. So your kindness will be meaningful and make so much more of a difference.

ONE MORE THING TO REMEMBER... and this is important!

EMPATHY IS A LIFE SKILL

Some people think empathy is a fluffy, cuddly 'nice-to-have'. And look, there is absolutely nothing wrong with fluffy, cuddly things (take Rahul's floofy one-eared bunny, for instance!) but empathy isn't fluffy or cuddly. Empathy is a **LIFE SKILL**. That means it's something you have to practise, something you have to think about and choose to do. It affects **ALL** our relationships with **ALL** the people around us and it can be a huge **FORCE FOR GOOD IN THE WORLD**. And it makes a difference in so many places!

Let's take a quick look at some of these places now.

EMPATHY IN RELATIONSHIPS

Whether with friends or family, relationships can get tricky when people don't understand each other's feelings and needs. But, when you use your empathy superpower, you stop thinking, "Me, me, me!" and start thinking about another person - even if you disagree with them. Understanding someone else's point of view will bring you closer together. It will help you to work things out in a way that is **OK** for everyone. Remember, empathy is about being there for and supporting each other. In a world where studies show that over one in four people **(ONE IN FOUR!!!!!)** feels lonely some of the time, this kind of connection has never been more important.

EMPATHY AT SCHOOL

All the relationship stuff above applies here too, because school (and home school!) is full of relationships. Did you know that children who have a stronger empathy superpower also do **BETTER** at school and are more successful in life? **CHECK IT OUT!**

Empathy is also absolutely key to our wellbeing and mental health, some of **THE** most important things **EVER**. We may not talk about them enough, but they're the foundation that everything else builds on. And guess what? As well as being super helpful at school, all of this stuff will carry you right the way through the world of work! See?

EMPATHY MAKES YOU A BETTER:

problem-solver

critical thinker

team player and friend

leader

EMPATHY = an **AMAZING** life skill.

And it's one we can **ALL** get really good at!

"To be a successful human being, you need to be in touch with other people's feelings."

JACQUELINE WILSON

EMPATHY IN THE COMMUNITY

Empathy transforms communities. Instead of creating divisions, it makes us want to reach out and build bridges. It makes us feel more connected. We start to really notice the people around us. We think more (and learn more) about who they are, and how they might feel. Empathy encourages us to be kinder and inspires us to make a difference in our community – to make everyone feel welcome and to help each other out wherever we can.

EMPATHY AND OUR PLANET

Empathy is an extraordinary superpower. You can have empathy for one person, or for a group of people, or for your local community, or – stretching even further – for our whole **PLANET!**

You see, your empathy superpower doesn't just help you to understand other people. It can grow into care for our planet (and all life on our planet too). That, in turn, will help you to see why it's important to do your little bit to look after our Earth and all its creatures.

Perhaps it's keeping your community clean, stopping food waste, fundraising for and donating to good causes, saving electricity, saving water, saving the bees or speaking out to raise awareness about climate change. Or maybe you learn something you never knew before about a particular group of people or part of the world, and your empathy superpower kicks in. From there, it's just one more step to take action in real life!

A DIP IN EMPATHY

We've looked at the power of empathy, but what happens when there isn't enough of it? That's when we end up with things like discrimination, bullying, even war. And, when grown-ups today don't feel enough empathy with our planet or with future generations, they feel less motivated to properly tackle the crisis of climate change.

Unfortunately, this is something that gets talked about a lot. (SORRY to be doom-and-gloomy!) People are worried that we're seeing a real dip in empathy. But here are two things to give you some hope.

Firstly, wherever there is a lack of empathy in the world or in a community, look closely. You'll also find empathy heroes doing everything they can to help. And secondly, YOU can be an empathy hero too! That's what you're doing already, by building your empathy superpower.

EMPATHY-BOOSTING ACTIVITIES

BOOK CHARACTERS ON HOLIDAY!

This activity will really help you to stand in a book character's shoes. Or flip-flops. Or snuggly slippers. Or soft, padded paws! (But not literally – it's just an expression that means imagining someone else's point of view!)

You will need a postcard or a piece of paper, and something to write and draw with.

IMAGINE the holidays of your favourite characters. Where would they go? What would they do? Think about what they are like and what they love doing. Where would Winnie-the-Pooh go? What about the skeletons in the Funnybones family?

DRAW the photos your characters would take on holiday. Write the postcard they might send home. Who would they write to? What would they say they'd been doing?

USE EMPATHY TO REWRITE THE NEWS

RAHUL NEWS

In the news, we see some amazing acts of empathy – but we also see a lot of cruelty, selfishness and injustice. How could the world be different? Well, one way to imagine it is by rewriting the news!

For this activity, you will need magazines, newspapers or a children's news show.

First, watch the news or read a newspaper or magazine together with a grown-up or your class.

Next, choose one news story to focus on. Think about how things could have been different if those involved had used their EMPATHY SUPERPOWER.

RAHUL SAVES ORANGUTANS

Now, rewrite the story with a big splash of EMPATHY in the mix! How different could things be?

SUPERPOWER CHECK-IN

Look at you! You've completed the very first step in developing your empathy superpower. You now know what empathy is and what it isn't. You know how it's different from sympathy, kindness and fixing stuff. You know it's an **AMAZING LIFE SKILL** and the starting point that helps you to feel inspired to make a difference in someone else's life or in the wider world. **AND** you know that reading is a pretty awesome way to boost it!

Next stop, **STEP 2**: understanding how empathy works in humans. In other words, time to get into the **SCIENCE!** Grab your lab coat, and we'll meet you on the next page!

STEP 2:

KNOW HOW EMPATHY WORKS

Now you know what empathy actually is, we can get into how it works. And **THAT** means getting into the **SCIENCE** of it all – specifically, the neuroscience. That's the study of our whole nervous system, especially our **BRAIN** and how it works. We can use it to shine a light on what happens inside us when we use our empathy superpower.

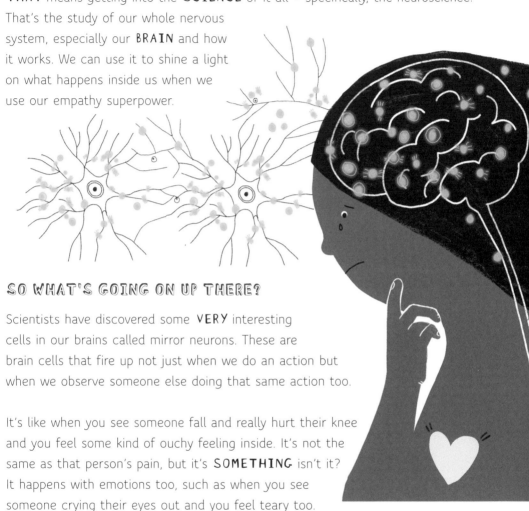

SO WHAT'S GOING ON UP THERE?

Scientists have discovered some **VERY** interesting cells in our brains called mirror neurons. These are brain cells that fire up not just when we do an action but when we observe someone else doing that same action too.

It's like when you see someone fall and really hurt their knee and you feel some kind of ouchy feeling inside. It's not the same as that person's pain, but it's **SOMETHING** isn't it? It happens with emotions too, such as when you see someone crying their eyes out and you feel teary too.

We don't just **SEE** other people's pain. We **FEEL** it. That's how we're wired. And you know what? This effect is stronger with people who have a stronger empathy superpower. Not only that – it's stronger when you actively **DECIDE** you're going to be more empathetic. Which is something all of us can do! Some scientists believe that this incredible mirroring ability is one of the key building blocks of empathy. It's not everything, but it's a pretty awesome start!

YOUR FANTASTIC PLASTIC BRAIN

Good news! Empathy is a skill you can **LEARN**. It's not like you're born with just one bag of empathy and that's your lot! Empathy is something that pretty much all of us can get **BETTER** at.

And the thing that makes it possible to learn about and boost your empathy superpower is your fantastic **PLASTIC** brain. No, not that kind of plastic! That would be **VERY** strange! Nope. Your brain is nice and soft and squishy and spongy, don't worry. When we talk about brain **PLASTICITY** (or neuroplasticity - now there's a word to impress people with!), we're talking about the brain's ability to rewire itself. To learn and adapt. In science-y terms, all those neurons (brain cells) that fire off when we use empathy could become stronger. The connections between various neurons become stronger too. And new ones are created. So, just by using your empathy superpower, you can give it a **SUPER-BOOST!**

A READER'S BRAIN

We've already talked about the power of **READING** and connecting with a character in the pages of a book. We're often good at this, and we do it when we watch movies too! What's more, as we now know, it's something we can get even **BETTER** at.

Scientists have actually scanned people's brains to see how they respond to stories, and they discovered something **FASCINATING**. When we read simple facts, we activate the bits of our brain that process language and words. Makes sense. No biggie. But then there's this: when we read a story, many more areas of the brain light up...

Why? Well, as we become more and **MORE** involved in a story and its characters, our mirror neurons get to work. So, when we're reading about a character running through the jungle or kicking a ball, the bits of our brain that have to do with those same activities can get fired up.

It's the same with textures and smells and other delicious descriptions that draw on our senses. When we read words like 'a velvet voice' or 'lavender' or 'soap', or when we read about food in a story – like chocolate cake or hot buttered toast – the bits of our brain that respond to those things in real life wake up. I bet they'd definitely be waking up if you read about some particularly pongy **CHEESY FEET!**

When we're wrapped up in a story, it's as if we're right there with the characters, experiencing their feelings. It's as if they and their feelings are real – we often don't just feel it in our imaginations, but in our actual **BODIES** too!

STIRRED UP BY STORIES

There's something else that happens when we follow a character's journey through all the **UPS** and **DOWNS** of a juicy story: our hormones kick in! Hormones are handy things that some parts of the body make in order to help other parts do their job.

Challenges (Cortisol)

Something **BIG** happens

OXYTOCIN:

Sometimes called the love hormone, oxytocin helps you to create a deep connection with a character. It means you care about them. You're on their TEAM! You feel with them and you want them to succeed!

CORTISOL:

Also known as the stress hormone, this one floods your body when you're worried about a character and the challenges they face, especially when things go wrong for them. "WHY is this happening?" you ask. "Will they make it through? What if they don't?!" You might even notice your body getting tense. Are you gripping the book tighter, staring harder, grinding your teeth or clenching your jaw? Hello, cortisol! (And hey, relax that jaw!)

Dopamine is released
as the story ends and
we leave feeling good.

Character overcomes biggest obstacle

DOPAMINE:

This one's the **feel-good hormone,** and it floods your brain when the main character overcomes the villain at the end of the story. (YESSSS!) Happy endings crank up the dopamine. In fact, even stories with a bittersweet ending can leave you with SOME kind of warm, fuzzy, hopeful feeling deep in your heart. That's dopamine at work too. And there's more! Dopamine is also linked to curiosity, creativity and LEARNING. So that incredible end-of-the-story space can be a very special spot to PAUSE and REFLECT on everything, and to give your empathy superpower a great big boost.

A STORY IS A STORY

It's not just made-up stories that make us feel this way. Non-fiction or factual books – true stories about the real world – can have a powerful empathy-boosting effect too.

Whenever we open up a book, we are entering another world. That incredible light show in our brain? It doesn't distinguish between true stories and fictional ones. A story is a story, as long as it's told in a way that moves us.

Amazing non-fiction books can open our minds and our hearts just as fiction does. They can change our attitudes and our behaviour too.

A TEENSY SHOUT-OUT FOR FUNNY BOOKS

Heart-crunchingly emotional stories can stir up empathy in us. But a book that makes us **SNORT**-laugh and splutter and cough and cry happy tears can do it too! It's not so much about the kind of book we're reading as it is about the connections we make with the characters. Fabulously funny books can pull us right into the story and give our empathy muscles a full-on workout. Also, funny and sad actually often go together: a story can be both totally hilarious and completely heart-breaking (and those are probably some of the best stories). And, either way, we can learn a **LOT** from them, because funny stories are often **STICKY** stories — they stick with us!

FROM READING TO THE REAL WORLD

So, now you know that your brilliant brain lights up when you read, and fires off as if you're actually part of the story. Here's the really interesting bit: that means you can use stories to experience lives you haven't lived yourself. You can explore and understand tricky feelings - such as jealousy, guilt, fear or loneliness - and big, important life events and challenges you've never faced yourself. And you get to do it all in **SAFE MODE**, tucked away in the pages of a book!

AND THEN... you can use everything you learn in the real world to:

☆ better understand other people

☆ break down barriers

☆ build better relationships

☆ be a better world citizen.

"Reading for empathy is like Lego. It helps you build and play around with an infinite number of scenarios involving yourself and others, all at your fingertips!"

SUE CHEUNG

Your brain = a top-class virtual reality machine

Psychology Professor Keith Oatley has called reading "the mind's flight simulator". In other words, reading is like running a computer simulation or a virtual reality video game in your **BRAIN**.

So, basically, your brain is this amazing, immersive gaming machine that is **SO** good at what it does that it all feels **REAL**.

NIIIIICE.

WOW.

Simulations are so important for learning. They're used for all sorts of things, from learning how to fly an aircraft or spacecraft to exploring big, complicated questions in science and politics. The reason simulations are so useful is because they provide a safe training ground for people to practise and make mistakes and learn and grow without hurting anyone.

That simulation we run when we read books? It's a **SUPER** way to work our empathy muscle in a safe space. Research shows that this process of reflecting on book characters and their dreams and fears and frustrations actually helps us to change our attitudes towards other people in the real world, and it also helps us to hone our real-life social skills!

READ → REFLECT → ACT

Read: Read books. **FEEL** with the characters!

Reflect: **THINK** about the characters' feelings and points of view. Really understand them.

Act: Be inspired to **ACT**. Turn empathy into action by doing some good in the world.

Look at Rahul. He's been reading a story about a kid who feels left out at school, and that's inspired him to do everything he can to make sure everyone around him feels included. When he understood what the lonely kid was going through, he didn't like the feeling of being left out, and he didn't want anyone else to feel that way either.

Big or small, empathy-inspired action makes a difference. TRUE superhero-style.

MOVIE TIME!

Studies show that watching movies can also boost your empathy superpower! In a great movie, you feel with the characters, and follow their journeys every step of the way.

And, when you read books, you use even more creative power because you're working your IMAGINATION by creating the characters in your MIND.

EMPATHY-BOOSTING ACTIVITIES
EMPATHY GLASSES

Make your own Empathy Glasses to help you to see the world from a book character's point of view! Look at these supremely snazzy ones designed by author-illustrator Jen Carney for inspiration. You can trace these glasses for inspiration, or design your own pair!

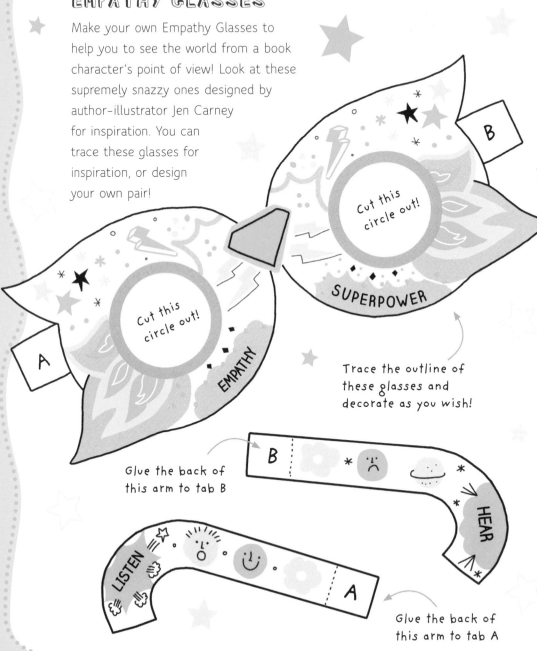

Cut this circle out!

B

SUPERPOWER

Cut this circle out!

A

EMPATHY

Trace the outline of these glasses and decorate as you wish!

Glue the back of this arm to tab B

B

HEAR

LISTEN

A

Glue the back of this arm to tab A

You will need some paper, something to draw with and a pair of scissors.

First, draw some glasses on a piece of paper, then cut them out, carefully cutting out holes for the eyes. You can add your own amazing designs and colour them in any way you like! **THEN**, it's time to put those glasses on and put them to use!

GO WILD!

Think about your favourite book characters. What is it that you remember about them? If you met that character, what would you chat about? What would they say to you? How would they behave? With your amazing Empathy Glasses on, **IMAGINE** what it's like to **BE** them and experience the world the way they do!

"A good way to help boost your empathy skills is to stop and think before you criticize someone who has made a mistake. If your teammate misses a penalty, if your baby sister breaks your toy by accident, if your classmate gives a wrong answer in class, put on your Empathy Glasses. They'll help you to understand how that person might be feeling, and how you might feel in their situation. That's empathy. And when people show empathy, the world is a kinder place."

JEN CARNEY

EMPATHY BOOKMARKS

For this activity, you'll need paper, scissors and something to draw and write with.

Can you think of a book character who is amazing at using their empathy superpower? Someone who really thinks about and understands other people and how they feel, and really cares about others? Draw a bookmark with a picture of that character and the name of the book they come from.

Maybe you can think of someone who might like this character and their story? If so, maybe you could give them this bookmark? You could even do a bookmark swap!

ROSE
YOU ARE A SUPERHERO.

SUPERPOWER CHECK-IN

That's **STEP 2**! So, as well as knowing what empathy **IS**, you also know how it actually **WORKS** in humans! You've got the science under your belt, so you really, truly understand it. And you know that, thanks to your fantastic **PLASTIC** brain, empathy is something you can always get better at! It's a muscle you can use and grow!

That's exactly what you're going to be doing in the next step: flexing that empathy muscle! Because **STEP 3** is all about **GETTING OUT THERE AND USING EMPATHY IN THE WILD.**

43

STEP 3:

USE YOUR EMPATHY OUT IN THE WILD

EMPATHY WALKS

So far, we've been doing quite a bit of chatting. Which is OK. We've been busy wrapping our brains around a big topic – empathy – and what it is, why it's so amazing and the science of how it works in us humans. We've even tried a few activities to get that empathy muscle working. But **NOW** it's time to take it out into the **WILD!**

An Empathy Walk is where you take a short trip around your local area and, as you go, you **IMAGINE** what it might be like to be the people you see, or to experience the situations you come across. You don't even have to actually walk. Do whatever works best for you. The main thing is to stay switched on when you're out and about. Take the time to really notice what is happening in your community. Imagine what it's like for those around you. To help with this, you can do something called an **Empathy 360**.

45

EMPATHY 360 DEGREES

To help with this, you can do something called an Empathy 360.

360 degrees is one whole turn. A full circle! Looking ALL around you!

1. SWITCH ON your empathy superpower.

2. REALLY LOOK around you.

3. WHO do you see?

OUCH!

6. DECIDE what **YOU** can do to make a difference.

5. REFLECT on your shiny new, all-round, 360-degree view.

4. IMAGINE things from another person's point of view.

Those last two bits are important. That's where you practise seeing things from another person's point of view, and **THEN** you turn empathy into **ACTION**. You use what you learn to see where you might be able to help in your own small but special superhero-y way.

AUTHORS AND ILLUSTRATORS IN THE WILD!

You can find lots of videos of authors and illustrators doing Empathy Walks over on the EmpathyLab website. Go to empathylab.uk/empathy-walk. (You'll also get to read some snippets from those walks in the quotes in this part of the book!)

ONE THING, TWO POINTS OF VIEW

While you are on your Empathy Walk, think about how things might affect people differently. Notice how the same thing might make one person feel one way, but it might make someone else feel something completely different. This is exactly what Welsh author Manon Steffan Ros discovered on her Empathy Walk.

"I look out over the train tracks, the way they stretch like a pointing finger towards the hills. I know there are people on the departing trains who wish they didn't have to go. And I know that there are people who watch the trains, wishing they could jump on board and leave. That must be really hard."

MANON STEFFAN ROS

AN EMPATHY WALK WITH THE SHARMAS

Oh look! The Sharmas have just been out for an Empathy Walk! Let's have a little snoop at what they discovered, shall we?

A BIN-COLLECTION LORRY:

The Sharmas heard the chug-chug-EEEEEK-crunch of the lorry before they saw it. The lorry made them remember all the people who have kept working through the pandemic, and the people who help us all year round in rain and snow and fierce, icy winds that whack you right in the face. They thought about how hard it must be some days, trudging through terrible weather to handle all that stinky rubbish. They wondered how many times people say "thank you" for all this work.

LITTER ON A BENCH:

The Sharmas noticed some crushed cans on a park bench. Who left them there? Why hadn't they put them in the bin right next to the bench? Were they in a hurry? Did they forget? Did they not think it was important? Someone would have to clear the cans up and, when the Sharmas thought about that, they decided to do it themselves.

Then Isha noticed a silver plaque on the bench: "In memory of Charlie Smith. Never forgotten." They all sat together for a little while, holding hands, wondering who Charlie was and thinking about how appreciated Charlie must have been.

BIRDSONG:

They heard the sweet sound of birdsong coming from the trees along with a gentle flutter of wings. They looked back at the busy street and wondered how often people stopped to listen to it. They wondered where everyone was rushing to. No time to pause. They thought about the birds and all they see from up there in the trees and the sky. When they crook their little heads, what are they thinking?

TWO PEOPLE ARGUING IN THE STREET: The Sharmas imagined being in this situation, with people walking past and not being able to resist peeking. How would that feel? They thought about how there must be two sides to the argument, and a whole backstory that no one knows other than those two people.

A BABY IN A PRAM: A grown-up was busy rummaging for something in their bag and the baby was crying its little heart out, then an older child (maybe a big brother?) reached into the pram to hold the baby's hand. The baby's crying really tugged at the Sharmas' hearts, but seeing the older child step in was so beautiful. They thought about how much love the older child must have for that baby. They also noticed how stressed and frazzled the grown-up looked. Maybe they had lost their keys? Or something else important?

THE LIBRARY: When the Sharmas looked through the windows of the library, they saw an old man wrapped up in a bobbly woollen scarf and a thick coat, rubbing his hands together. It was freezing cold outside, but the library was warm and welcoming. The Sharmas thought about how expensive it is to heat your home. Did the old man come to the library to find some warmth? Did he even have a home? It reminded the Sharmas that no one ever really knows what someone else is dealing with.

Then they saw a smiling librarian helping a child to find a book. What kinds of things would the child enjoy, they wondered? The librarian handed the child a comic, and the Sharmas noticed how the child's eyes lit up like bright stars in a night sky and the librarian looked so happy.

AFTER YOUR EMPATHY WALK

Here are some different ways to **REFLECT** on what you have seen and experienced.

TALK IT THROUGH:

Of course you'll talk as you go along (you're allowed to!), but have a chat afterwards too. Share stories of what you saw and experienced and learned.

MAP IT OUT:
You might want to draw a simple map of your Empathy Walk. Don't put in any street names or anything that might identify your area. Instead, add some drawings and notes to show what you spotted along the way. Like this one here:

DOODLE AWAY:
Set your inner artist free, and draw or doodle some of the things you saw. You could even sketch some scenes or make a comic strip!

GET WRITING:

You might want to turn your thoughts and discoveries and feelings into a poem or a play or some other piece of writing. It's up to you!

MAKE A FILM: You might decide to make a mini-film of your Empathy Walk or a collage of photos. (But please make sure you don't take pictures of other people or private property without permission!)

GET INSPIRED!

Is there something you noticed on your walk that **INSPIRED** you to take action? Perhaps you spotted litter scattered across the street and that made you determined to pick some up? Or maybe, like the Sharmas, you saw a bin-collection lorry and decided to make extra-specially sure to always say "thank you" to the workers whenever you see them?

THANK YOU!

Empathy is an incredible superpower but, as the saying goes, "With great power comes great responsibility." How will **YOU** use your empathy superpower to make a difference in the world?

"I'm actually a postman as well as being an author. I conduct Empathy Walks five days a week. Being a postman actually requires an enormous amount of empathy. You need a base level of empathy not to trample people's gardens and flowers! And you have to be aware that the things you're delivering could be life-changing to people. They could be bringing incredible good news; they could be bringing horrible bad news. You just don't know what you're putting through people's doors."

BEN DAVIS

EMPATHY-BOOSTING ACTIVITIES
WHIP OUT THOSE EMPATHY GLASSES

You made some awesome Empathy Glasses in **STEP 2** (page 40).
If you didn't, you can flick back to that
activity and give it a go now.

As well as using
your Empathy Glasses
to step into the
worlds of your favourite
characters, you can also
use them to see things from
the points of view of the people in
your community. Can you use them
to really understand some of the
people who live and work around
you? Maybe some of the people you
spotted on your Empathy Walk?

SEEK OUT SOME EMPATHY HEROES

Did you know that our world is full of people who are really **GREAT** at using their empathy superpower? Let's find some from your local community together!

For this activity, you will need some local newspapers, magazines, websites or children's news shows.

Look in all the different news sources you can find for empathy heroes near you. Talk about what makes these people empathy heroes, why they do what they do and what a difference they make. Maybe you can think up a way to thank them or celebrate them and spread the word about what they do!

SUPERPOWER CHECK-IN

And that's **STEP 3** done!

BOOM!

So, to recap:

⭐ you know what empathy is

⭐ you know how it works in the human brain

⭐ you've taken it for a spin in the real world.

What's next? It's a biggie: naming, knowing and spotting **EMOTIONS**. Are you ready? Let's **GO**!

"At the moment, dandelions are everywhere, but we often ignore them. But they're this massive splash of yellow and orange. If you look up dandelions... they're tough and they're persistent and they push their roots into tiny spaces. It makes you think about the people that survive on the edges. The people we don't see, even though they're very much there, who are trying to survive, trying to push their roots down, trying to exist."

PATRICE LAWRENCE

STEP 4:
LEARN TO RECOGNIZE EMOTIONS

Wowzers! We're past the halfway mark. **HIGH-FIVE,** my friends! We're getting deep into it now. So, we've been looking at ways to see things from other people's points of view, but the focus for this step is **EMOTIONS.**

Specifically, we're going to look at how to:

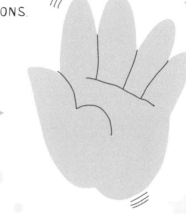

★ name them

✹ understand them

★ spot them in others

EMPATHY is being able to experience and understand other people's emotions and feelings and their points of view.

So... er... what are emotions? And what's the difference between **EMOTIONS** and **FEELINGS?** This is going to get a **TEENSY** bit messy, but hang in there, **OK?** You see, the experts haven't exactly agreed on the difference – but many say that emotions are our raw and instant response to something, while feelings are what come afterwards.

For example, if you paint your best picture **EVER**, then accidentally spill water all over it, your first reaction might be **ANGER**. Yep, that burning emotion. Can you imagine it filling up your whole body, maybe? But then, after a couple more seconds, you might have a whole bunch of other feelings about what just happened. You might feel **FRUSTRATED** or **ANNOYED** or **REGRETFUL**.

There are so many words to describe how we feel, and we'll get to that in just a moment. But for now, let's just take a closer look at that crunching, sweaty, red-hot rage when you ruin your own painting. It's an example of how an emotion – in this case anger – can get bundled up with actual changes in your body.

There are other emotions that can change your body in other ways. Maybe when you're scared, your breath becomes shallow and your heart starts pounding in your chest. You might even feel some full-on swirly-whirly weirdness in your tummy. But when you're feeling calm, you can take long, deep breaths and your body feels soft and comfy and not tense at all. It's nice and relaxed.

Have you noticed these sorts of feelings in your body? What's **THAT** about?

THE SCIENCE OF EMOTIONS

If you want, you can think of your brain as some kind of wizard, always busy mixing up potions. **EMOTION** potions. These chemical concoctions send messages throughout your body, and they're not just for fun, either. They have an important purpose...

"AHEM! MAY I HAVE YOUR ATTENTION, PLEASE!"

Suppose your brain senses danger. Way back in the days of the earliest humans, danger might have come in the form of a bear or a crocodile, but today it might be something like a really tricky test or crossing a super busy road. Well, to your brain, it doesn't really matter whether you're facing a bear or a test – when it senses any sort of danger, your brain floods your system with the stress hormone cortisol (remember, from page 32?). It also pumps out some adrenaline, another type of hormone, which keeps you **AWAKE** and **ALERT** and **READY TO ACT**. And what's the other thing you feel while the cortisol and the adrenaline are swooshing about? That's right: **FEAR**. Then, when the danger passes, your brain will send out a calming mix of hormones to turn things down a notch or two.

"Books can be maps that help us navigate some of the most tricky emotional places!"

NADIA SHIREEN

YOUR EMOTIONAL VOCABULARY

When you're in a whirlwind of emotion, you can get overwhelmed and feel out of control. It's hard, isn't it? We've all been there!

Well, here's something a little bit wonderful: if you can name an emotion, you can take back some control. You can figure things out. You can step back and observe your emotions instead of just being all tangled up in them. It also means you can discuss them with someone else, and get help if you need it. That's important.

All you need to do is E−X−P−A−N−D your emotional vocabulary!

You can move beyond basic words like: sad, happy, angry, scared and surprised.

Here are just a few words for emotions and
feelings. How many do you recognize?
How many can you add to this list?

HAPPY

cheerful
delighted
jubilant
ecstatic
elated
excited
joyful
overjoyed
uplifted
merry
contented
calm
pleased

ANGRY

scared
furious
irate
cross
frustrated
incensed
enraged
outraged
exasperated
infuriated
annoyed
irritated

shy   grouchy   bitt

SAD

unhappy
sorrowful
miserable
dejected
gloomy
glum
depressed
heartbroken
hopeless
hurt
sorry
regretful
apologetic

SCARED

resentful
frightened
afraid
anxious
fearful
apprehensive
terrified
petrified
nervous
worried
panicky
flustered
frazzled

SURPRISED

stunned
shocked
startled
confused
baffled
unsure
uncertain
perplexed
astonished
amazed

OTHER WORDS

self-conscious

embarrassed   disgusted   sickened   inquisitive

satisfied   grumpy   curious   interested   proud

grateful   wistful   bored   inspired

awkward

ealous   lonely   playful   disinterested   67

BIG EMOTIONS

Naming big, overwhelming emotions in particular can help you to turn the dial down on their intensity. It can help you to calm down enough to figure out what to do next, or how to deal with a challenge.

And **HEY!** If you get extra-specially good at recognizing and understanding and naming your **OWN** emotions, then guess what? It means you'll get even better at recognizing and understanding them in other people too.

SPOTTING THE SIGNS

You can sometimes get a sense of how other people are feeling by looking at the expressions on their faces or what they are doing with their bodies. This isn't always the case, mind you, but it can be!

Have a look at the Sharmas.
Can you guess what they're feeling?

How about now? What does
their body language tell you?

69

You know what you were doing just there? You were using your empathy superpower to look at these pictures and **IMAGINE** how Shivani, Isha and Rahul might be feeling.

Research has shown that, when it comes to basic emotions, our facial expressions and body language are *often* similar, no matter who we are or where we're from. **BUT**. Watch out! It's not always as simple as looking at someone's face or their body. Humans are seriously **COMPLICATED!** Each of us is unique. We have our own special way of expressing our feelings. We don't come with a manual on 'The Correct Way to Display Emotions'.

So you have to pay attention to a mix of things - facial expressions, body language, what a person says and does **AND** whatever else is going on.

EMPATHY AND AUTISM

"One of the most widely
known and damaging stereotypes
about autism is that autistic
people aren't empathetic.
Firstly – every autistic person
is different, so generalizing
is never helpful. And secondly
– many of us are extremely
empathetic and can even absorb
the emotions of others due to our
sensory sensitivities. Everyone
expresses emotion differently
and there is no right or wrong
way to show empathy."

ABIGAIL BALFE

FINDING FEELINGS IN BOOKS

In **STEP 3**, we talked about how books are a kind of **SAFE MODE** for working our empathy muscle. They also help us to get to grips with emotions.

Picture books are amazing for this. You're never too old for picture books. **NEVER**. They're mini-masterpieces. So much story in just a few pages, and it's not just the words doing the telling – it's the pictures too. It's also the **SPACE** picture books leave for **YOU**, the reader, to fill in with your wonderful imagination. The space they leave for you to use your empathy superpower.

There are plenty of picture books about big emotions, such as *Barbara Throws a Wobbler* by Nadia Shireen, where Barbara, a little cat, is in an **ABSOLUTE MOOOOD**. Or *The Invisible* by Tom Percival, which explores all sorts of feelings brought up for a family who don't have enough money and are finding it hard to get by.

But you can use **ALL KINDS** of picture books as a safe space to imagine how characters are feeling. Take *Supertato* by Sue Hendra and Paul Linnet: when Evil Pea is up to no good in the supermarket, the fruits and veggies are **EXTREMELY** worried. Then, when Supertato saves the day, they're so relieved and happy. You can switch points of view, too, and think about the villain of the story, if there is one (it's Evil Pea, in this case). Ask yourself, "What's cooking in that brain? Why does the villain do what they do?"

In picture books, comics and other illustrated books, you can look closely at the pictures and study the characters' expressions and body language. You don't always need the text to tell you what's going on. Some books, such as Shaun Tan's *The Arrival*, don't have any words at all, but you can still follow the characters and use your empathy superpower to zoom in on their emotional journeys.

Sometimes, the pictures tell a completely different story from the words, so **YOU** (being the supremely *clever* reader you are) might **GET** something that the storyteller totally misses!

BE AN EMOTIONS DETECTIVE

You can play this game with **ANY** book. Go on a feelings hunt. Think about the characters and their emotions at different stages in the story. Discuss those emotions with a grown-up or with a friend. Why do these characters feel the way they do? What's happening?

How can you tell what a character is feeling? Is it what they say or what they do? If there are pictures, is it something in their expressions or body language? If there aren't any pictures, is it how the author describes things?

FOR EXAMPLE...

In *The Lost Whale* by Hannah Gold, you could look at the wonder Rio feels when he first sees the magnificent grey whale, and the beautiful connection he starts to feel with her.

In *Danny Chung Does Not Do Maths* by Maisie Chan, you could look at how disappointed Danny feels (at first) when the **BIG SURPRISE** his parents promised him is definitely *surprising* but **TOTALLY** not what he wanted and turns his whole life upside down.

In *Emmy Levels Up* by Helen Harvey, you could think about how crushed Emmy feels when the other girls are making fun of her trainers and her second-hand jacket. The book says her chest feels tight. What emotion do you think she's experiencing? Can you zoom in on it?

Have a go at playing emotions detective with other books that you read!

You might spot some characters that hide their emotions. In *Jelly* by Jo Cotterill, the main character, Jelly, pretends to be all confident on the outside when, deep inside, it's a very different story.

You'll meet some characters dealing with BIG emotions. In *Onyeka and the Academy of the Sun* by Tolá Okogwu, Onyeka has an extremely awesome power, but to use it, she has to learn to accept her emotions and channel them.

You might even discover some characters who find it REALLY hard to understand their own emotions - and other people's too! In *Loki: A Bad God's Guide to Being Good* by Louie Stowell, the god of mischief has been banished to Earth and is stuck in the body of an 11-year-old boy. He has just 30 days to learn how to be empathetic and kind or VERY BAD **THINGS WILL HAPPEN TO HIM**. At the start, he struggles to notice his own feelings and he has a **MEGA** hard time understanding how the people around him feel. He may be a Norse **GOD**, but he hasn't figured out his empathy superpower yet. (Well, look at that. You're a step ahead of Loki! **GO, YOU!**)

POETRY

Poems are another safe space to help you to learn about emotions. They're just stories in another form, really. They're also a wonderful way to EXPRESS your feelings. And, let me tell you, that's WAY better (and healthier) than bottling them up. Writing poems lets you dive deep into your feelings. It lets you take a good look at them. If they're not-so-nice feelings, it can help them to feel less FOREVER-Y. And if they're nice feelings, capturing them in a poem means you can always go back to them for a BOOST.

EMPATHY- BOOSTING BOOKS

Every year, EmpathyLab puts together a collection of books that help to supercharge your empathy. It's called the Read for Empathy collection, and you'll find it at empathylab.uk.

There's something for everyone in there — fiction, facts, poetry — and for all ages too.

EMPATHY-BOOSTING ACTIVITIES

EMPATHY CHARADES

Try acting out different emotions using your facial expressions, and see if you can get someone else to guess what you are supposed to be feeling. Take turns being the person doing the acting and the person doing the guessing.

Now, try doing the same with body language!

BODY MIRRORING   Created by Jo Cotterill

This activity takes things even further! Think back to a time when you felt a really strong emotion. **ANY** emotion. What position were you in at the time? Can you remember? Without **SAYING** anything, get into that position. See if you can get someone else to guess how you were feeling by looking at your body language. Then let them copy your position exactly. When they get into that position, with their bodies in the same shape and their faces with the same expression as yours, ask them how they feel. Do they understand what it is that you were feeling? Have a go and see! Then swap roles and try it again.

Notice how **MIRRORING** someone's body and face can help you to feel the things that they are feeling? There's a sneaky bit of science behind this too (as always). It's because our brains send messages to our bodies, but our bodies **ALSO** send messages to our brains! (And **PSSST!** This is also why changing your body language can sometimes help you to change how you're feeling! How cool is that?)

SUPERPOWER CHECK-IN

Annnnnnnd that's **STEP 4 IN THE BAG**. Now you know how to recognize emotions in yourself, and you've got a whole bunch of incredible words you can use to name them. And, since you're so in tune with **YOUR** emotions and feelings, you're getting **VERY** good at recognizing them in other people too. You're making amazing progress! Your empathy superpower is just getting stronger and **STRONGER!** Now, let's take it to the next level. It's time to power up those communication skills.

STEP 5:

BE A
BRILLIANT
COMMUNICATOR

We've done quite a bit so far. You know what empathy is and how it works, you've taken your growing superpower out into the wild for a spin **AND** you're building up a pretty fabulous emotional vocabulary! Now it's time to talk **COMMUNICATION SKILLS**.

Being a brilliant communicator is all about getting really good at sharing your thoughts and feelings and ideas with someone else. It's a two-way thing: you share and so does the other person! It means that you can understand other people better, and that other people can understand you better.

Hopefully, some **HUUUGE** lights are flashing in your brain right now.

Remember that empathy is **ALL** about understanding other people's emotions, feelings and points of view? So, by boosting your communication skills, you're also boosting your empathy superpower!

Now, when you have a conversation with someone, there are two main bits: **TALKING** and **LISTENING**.

LISTENING LIKE A PRO

We all know how to listen, right? Welllllll... not always! Turns out that great listening isn't actually as simple as it might sound. You have to really pay attention and be genuinely interested in what someone has to say. You have to bring your empathy superpower to the party.

When you really listen, you aren't just waiting for your turn to speak. And you certainly don't look at the person who is speaking but secretly zone out to plan what YOU want to say next (or what you want to eat later).

You JUST... LISTEN!

That's it. That's all. LISTEN.

You pay attention to what the other person is telling you. You listen to the words they are saying, and you also notice their body language and their facial expressions. You give them time to say what they need without interrupting them.

Then, when they've finished talking, you show that you are truly listening by repeating what you have heard. Reflect it back to them – a bit like a mirror! Show them that you are interested and that you get what they are trying to say.

If you were sharing your thoughts or feelings with someone else, you'd want them to be interested in what you had to say, right? You'd want them focused on you and paying attention, rather than daydreaming about pizzas or scoring goals or thinking up some clever thing to say once you've **FINALLYYYYY** stopped talking?

Another thing you can do to show you are listening is ask questions to find out more. Just be careful not to make it seem like you're a pirate chucking questions at a prisoner about to walk the plank! You don't want to be rude or nosy or make the other person feel uncomfortable. **HOW** you ask matters. Ask in a gentle way that shows you care and that you're thinking about their feelings. And stop if they don't want to say any more.

In fact, let's see some super questioning in action by stepping into the story world of Little Red Riding Hood and the Wolf. (Turns out he's not keen on the 'Big Bad Wolf' thing, so yes, it's just the Wolf. Or Wolf. Wolfie when you become buddies.)

No, no, I WANT to... it's... so nice to be listened to. No one ever listens to me.

It's OK. You don't have to carry on talking if it's too hard.

It all started with that business with your GRANNY last week...

Hang on... my granny? What happened to my granny? She's OK, isn't she?

I'm alright dear, just had a close call with a wolf.

Gotta say I'm more than a BIT concerned about what Wolfie is hiding there... But did you notice how he felt when Red Riding Hood was listening to him?

Take a moment to think about how good **YOU** feel when you know that someone is really listening to you. You feel understood and respected and as though your thoughts and ideas are important, right? Isn't that something wonderful? And isn't it something worth sharing with others? Well, when you use your empathy superpower, you can do just that!

THE LOVELIEST LISTENING

Did you know that animals can be amazing listeners? If you have a pet or know someone who does, you may have noticed they'll sometimes sit quietly with their human friends. Just sitting. Being there. Listening to their friend. Because sometimes that's all it takes to make someone feel better. To feel cared for.

LISTENING = LEARNING

Listening is such an amazing way to learn about another human being. And humans are **FASCINATING**. They're living, breathing storybooks!

When someone shares something with you in a conversation, they're basically giving you an **EXPRESS TICKET** into their **BRAIN** and their **HEART**. So take the ticket and jump on the ride! It's just another way for you to use that empathy superpower of yours to understand their feelings and thoughts and points of view.

And do you want to know something really interesting? When you're a **PRO** at listening, people will share even more with you, because they'll feel safe and comfortable and cared for. So you'll learn even more! That'll bring you closer together too. All of this is true even if you're having a discussion where you disagree with the other person. You can still listen 100 per cent and learn a **LOT**. To be clear, that doesn't mean you can't call them out on things - it just means you can better understand where they are coming from.

ONE MORE THING: NOOOO FIXING!

Great listening isn't about rushing to give advice. In fact, one of the most important parts of great listening is the SPACE (and the SILENCE!) you give to others so they can work things out for themselves.

And look, I know that the silence bit is hard if you're a chatterbox like me! But think about it: when you have a problem, and you talk it through with someone who is really amazing at listening, the most helpful thing they can do is to HEAR you. They don't have to say anything, or give you ways to fix stuff. And actually, when they stay quiet for long enough for YOU to work things out, you usually DO! Working things out this way is really powerful, because no one knows you better than YOU do. Also, you might find it easier to take — and stick to — next steps that were your own idea in the first place.

Sometimes

you'll see a planet
standing by itself
in the corridor
between classes.

It has no sun to warm to
and no moon to sing to
so maybe it's lost or maybe
it's just waiting
for someone like you
to sometimes say hello,
how are you.

DOM CONLON

WHEN IT'S YOUR TURN TO TALK...

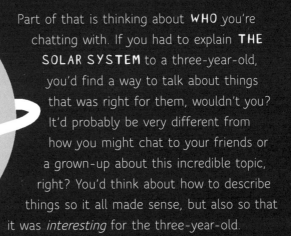

Part of that is thinking about **WHO** you're chatting with. If you had to explain **THE SOLAR SYSTEM** to a three-year-old, you'd find a way to talk about things that was right for them, wouldn't you? It'd probably be very different from how you might chat to your friends or a grown-up about this incredible topic, right? You'd think about how to describe things so it all made sense, but also so that it was *interesting* for the three-year-old.

I bet you do this **ALL** the time when you're speaking to different people about different things. Well, guess what? When you do, you're using your empathy superpower!

Understanding things from another person's point of view can also help you to find a reason for them to *care* about whatever it is that you have to say. When you do that, you're also using your empathy superpower!

What about when you think really carefully about how to say something so that you don't hurt someone else's feelings? Yep, that's your empathy superpower in play again!

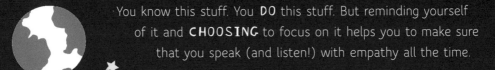

You know this stuff. You **DO** this stuff. But reminding yourself of it and **CHOOSING** to focus on it helps you to make sure that you speak (and listen!) with empathy all the time.

PEN PALS

Have you ever had a pen pal before? Someone to write to and receive letters or emails from? When you do, you get to put that PRO-level listening and talking to use! Pay attention to what your pen pal tells you. When you reply to them, show you've understood and that you're interested in them and what they have to say by asking good questions. And think about what they might like you to tell them.

BOOK TALK!

One way to polish those listening and speaking skills so they sparkle is by talking about – you guessed it! – **BOOKS**. When you get together with your friends or family to chat about what you're reading, you create a cosy space where everyone has a turn to share and to listen. So everyone gets a chance to use all the skills you've been learning about in this chapter!

You don't even have to all read the same book. Look at Isha. She's been chatting about books on video calls with her nani (her grandma) who's over in India. They're reading **VERY** different things, so they know **NOTHING** about what's going

on with the characters in each other's books. And it's **FINE!** It **WORKS!** It just means that Isha and her nani each have to do an awesome job of communicating what's happening in their book and what the characters are going through. And as listeners, they'll each have to do some supremely good listening too!

Now, when you're talking about books and taking turns to share and listen, there's one key thing to remember: **THERE IS NO RIGHT OR WRONG**. In fact, that's so important I'm going to say it again: **THERE IS NO RIGHT OR WRONG**.

Create a **NO JUDGEMENT ZONE** for your conversation. Be nice. Play nice. Listen to what others have to say, even if you disagree with them. Open your mind and be interested in what they have to say. Reflect back what you hear. Ask good questions to find out more about the characters **AND** to show that you really care (and haven't just zoned out, wondering what it might be like to live on Mars). Then, when it's your turn to share, think deeply about what the person you're talking to might like to hear about the book. Make it interesting for them.

So go ahead! Use all of the things we've talked about in this step to have a good old chat about books! Here are some questions you could ask.

★ Could you tell me about the story and the characters in it?

★ Which character stuck in your mind the most?

★ Was there a character you felt sad for or proud of or worried about?

★ Did any of the characters have really strong feelings? What words could you use to describe their feelings? (WHIP OUT YOUR SHINY, GROWING EMOTIONAL VOCABULARY HERE)

★ How did the characters' feelings change over the course of the book? (Yep, the reader's gotta REALLY pay attention for this one!) How did the characters feel at the start? How did they feel when things got tricky? Or when it seemed like ALL HOPE WAS LOST? How did they feel at the end?

★ Were there characters you found you understood easily? Were there any you struggled to understand? Did any of the characters surprise you?

★ Which characters in the book needed someone to show them empathy? And which characters were amazing empathy HEROES?

★ WHY do you think the characters behave the way they do?

★ If you could whoosh into the book, what questions would you ask the characters?

I wonder what they are wondering?

THE POWER OF "I WONDER"

When you're thinking and chatting about characters, there's a very cool trick you can use: have a WONDER. For instance, you could ask yourself, "I wonder WHY this character made the decision they did?" or, "I wonder WHY they behaved in that way?" Talk about what you would do if YOU were them. WONDER at it all. And of course you can do all of this for factual stories as well as made-up ones. There's PLENTY to wonder at and discover together when it comes to the REAL world and real people, events and ideas. It can make for some amazing conversations!

"I WONDER!"

"HMMMMM!"

SO... try it for yourself! Dive deep into the worlds you read about in books and brush up those communication skills!

And just so you don't forget (yes, I really am going to say it for a **THIRD** time): **THERE IS NO RIGHT OR WRONG.**

Take turns to share and listen to each other, and see how much you can **LEARN** and **GROW!**

"Why read books? Because books open our eyes and hearts and minds. They help us to see and feel and experience the world from other points of view. They are the greatest EMPATHY ENGINES ever invented!"

SF SAID

EMPATHY-BOOSTING ACTIVITIES

THE LISTENING SWITCH
Created by Jo Cotterill

Empathy

Buddy up with someone and take turns really **LISTENING** to each other. One person will be the listener and the other will be the sharer. You could even add a third person as an observer to watch the listening activity and see how you get on!

First, the listener imagines that they have a big listening switch in their brain. They turn it on so that they can listen 100 per cent. With **EMPATHY**.

Next, the sharer talks about something that has happened to them recently. It can be something tiny, but it should have made them **FEEL** something. It doesn't matter what they felt - it can be any emotion! They could even describe a moment in a book that made them feel something very strongly.

While the sharer is talking, the listener pays 100 per cent attention, listening like a **PRO**. Then, the listener reflects back what they have heard. For example, they might say, "So you felt disappointed, because you were really looking forward to eating that piece of cake after school, but when you got home it was all gone?"

THEN SWAP ROLES AND TRY AGAIN!

Afterwards, take some time to talk about how it felt being the listener and how it felt being the sharer. Think about how you can use this listening switch in **REAL LIFE** with your friends and family. What would the world be like if we **ALL** used our listening switches more often?

LISTENING VOUCHERS

We all have times when we just need someone to **REALLY** listen to us. So how about making some listening vouchers that you can whip out when you need them? A listening voucher is basically a sneaky way of reminding the listener (which could be **YOU!**) to turn on their listening switch.

Listening vouchers also make a lovely gift for friends and family members.

All you need is some paper and something to write and draw with. How you design your listening vouchers is totally up to you! Here's an example, to get you started.

HUMAN DISCOVERIES

The idea with this activity is to discover more about someone else and find a way to better understand each other.

You will need some paper, something to write with and maybe a jar or a little box (if you have one).

Buddy up again, and take turns being the listener and the sharer – but this time, use the set of listening prompts on the next page to learn more about each other. If you want, you can choose some prompts to write down, then put them in the jar or box and pull them out one at a time.

Take turns reading each prompt aloud and responding to it. Skip past anything that one of you feels uncomfortable with or doesn't want to talk about.

And remember to flip on that **LISTENING SWITCH!** What will you discover?

LISTENING PROMPTS

I'D LIKE TO HEAR ABOUT...

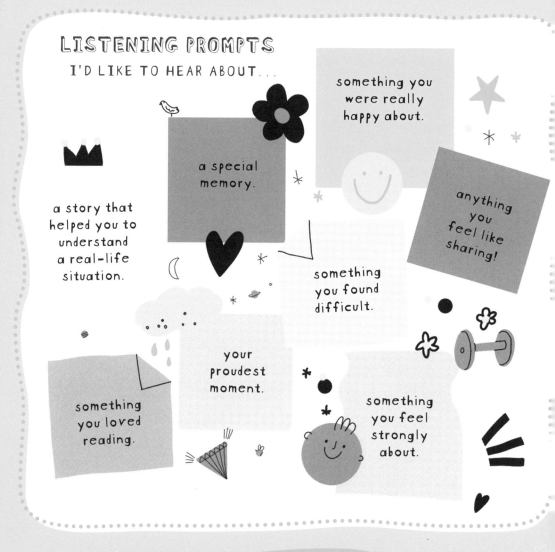

something you were really happy about.

a special memory.

a story that helped you to understand a real-life situation.

anything you feel like sharing!

something you found difficult.

your proudest moment.

something you loved reading.

something you feel strongly about.

SUPERPOWER CHECK-IN

That's **STEP 5** done and dusted! **CHECK OUT** your empathy superpower! Getting nice and strong there, isn't it, now that you've figured out how to be a **BRILLIANT** communicator who listens like a **PRO**?

The next step is more of a leap. A leap into building the **ATTITUDE** of an empathy hero. Are you ready? Of course you are! Let's go!

"The word empathy contains roots that mean 'affection' and 'suffering' and 'within'. When we empathize with others, the affection we feel teaches us how to carry their suffering within us. But it works both ways, together our suffering is halved and our affection doubled."

JOSEPH COELHO

STEP 6:

BECOME THE ULTIMATE EMPATHY HERO!

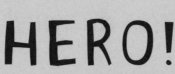

So here we are. At the final step.

It is **TIME**, my friends. Time to transform into a full-on **EMPATHY HERO**.

Now, being an empathy hero isn't about striking a pose or sticking on a cape (although I bet you'd look **DAZZLING** in a cape). It's about **ATTITUDE**. And it's about taking **ACTION**.

Wayyyy back in **STEP 1**, we talked about the three parts of empathy: **FEELING**, **THINKING** and **ACTING**. In this step, we're going to zoom in on that last bit! One way to do that is by making an **EMPATHY RESOLUTION** – a promise to **USE** your empathy superpower to make a difference in the world, however big or small. You'll spot some examples of real-life Empathy Resolutions made by actual children scattered about the following pages. Just a little something to inspire you! Like this one!

My Empathy Resolution is...
to really challenge myself
to understand other people's
points of view.

We'll come back to Empathy Resolutions in a bit, but **FIRST**...

LET'S TALK ABOUT ATTITUDE

ATTITUDE is how you think and feel about stuff, how you go about things in the world and, well, the *kind of person you are*! So what sort of attitude does an **EMPATHY HERO** have?

What do **YOU** think? Cover up the next bit and have a guess.

I'm serious. Cover it up.

In fact, I'll *help* you to cover it up by chucking in one of those Empathy Resolutions while you have a think! You've got this. I know you have!

My Empathy Resolution is... to be kind to everyone I meet. They might be going through a tough time.

OK, you're a **PRO** now, so you've probably come up with **LOTS** of wonderful ideas about what an empathy hero's attitude is like. Maybe your list includes things like:

★ thinking about other people instead of being all "Me, me, me!"

★ keeping that LISTENING SWITCH turned on

★ IMAGINING what things are like from someone else's point of view

★ THINKING about HOW other people feel and WHY they feel the things they do

★ UNDERSTANDING why others DO the things they do and why they BELIEVE the things they believe.

★ CARING about other people, as well as for our PLANET and all its amazing creatures

★ being INSPIRED to help however you can

★ feeling like it's your RESPONSIBILITY to make a difference.

And, to put the **HERO** in empathy hero, you might also have:

Empathy heroes **DO** all of these things, but not because they're born that way. Nope. It's because they have been working their empathy muscles **HARD**.

Empathy is a skill that they **CHOOSE** to use. And they use it *again* and *again* and *again*, until they do it almost without thinking.

I keep saying 'they', but what I really mean here is 'you'. Yes, YOU. You choose to use your empathy superpower every single time you try out one of the empathy-boosting activities in this book. You do it every time you WONDER about what the characters in a book - or people in the real world! - are thinking or feeling. You use it every time you listen or talk with empathy. And, every time you choose to use that empathy superpower, it becomes a stronger force inside you - and one day you'll find that you're using it *all the time*, without thinking much about it!

YOU ARE WHAT YOU BELIEVE YOU ARE

Here's something fascinating! Research shows that how we think about ourselves affects how we behave and how we interact with the world. People who think of themselves as being full of empathy end up being empathy heroes. They're more likely to use their empathy superpower to imagine how other people feel. They're more likely to try to help others, and they'll be quick to get in there too! So go ahead and remind yourself every single day that you ARE an empathy hero!

My Empathy Resolution is...
to support my friends when they are going through a hard time by just being there for them. Sometimes all people need is someone around them who they can talk to and trust. I want to try to be that person.

WE'RE ALL HEROES, REALLY

Every time you're inspired to turn empathy into **ACTION**, and every time you **USE** your empathy to make a difference for another person or for our planet or for the world's creatures, that's the empathy hero in you!

You *know* your inner empathy hero is there. Virtually all of us have one.

"Ummm... thank you??!!"

Think about little children. They often want to **HELP**, don't they? Even if 'helping' means accidentally making a humongous mess.

Most of the time, little children **WANT** to share stuff. I mean, sometimes they don't, but very often they **DO!** They like sharing and giving, whether it's a drippy half-chewed toy or a very dodgy-looking soggy cookie! But... er... it's the thought that counts, right?

Sharing stuff, along with working together and caring for each other, is part of being human. It might not always feel that way (especially with what we see and hear in the news!), but it's true. Studies show that actually, on the whole, many of us **DO** care about one another, and we **DO** want to be kind and helpful. It's just that we need to focus on that part of ourselves - we need to *choose* to use our empathy superpower. We need to work at it and make it stronger.

MY EMPATHY
RESOLUTION IS...
TO NOT JUDGE
PEOPLE BEFORE
GETTING TO KNOW
THEM.

Just like plants need food and water, your empathy superpower needs attention.

LITTLE THINGS MAKE A BIG DIFFERENCE

The difference an empathy hero makes doesn't have to be earth-shaking, mind-blowing, front-of-the-newspaper stuff. (Although, hey, it might be!) It can be little things around the house, at school or in the community.

Take the Sharmas. When Isha uses her empathy superpower to see things from Shivani's point of view, she understands that her mum is juggling a **LOT** on her own. So Isha decides to help out more at home by tidying up, putting away the shopping and folding the washing.

104

Meanwhile, Shivani realizes she hasn't exactly been listening 100 per cent to Isha and Rahul, because half her attention is usually on her **PHONE**. So she's going to chuck that phone (OK, not *really*, but she will set it aside!) and flip her listening switch on more often.

As for Rahul, that little dude thinks he could be a better listener too. For him, that means not **INTERRUPTING** all the time, even if he's **VERY** excited and absolutely **BURSTING** to say something!

Do you know what's really interesting about all these little steps? It's that they make a **BIG** difference to everyone's relationships. In the case of the Sharmas, they all take the time to understand each other better, and to try to make things easier for each other. **END RESULT**: they are *all* happier!

Just imagine what a **HUMONGOUS** difference tiny actions like these would make if everyone in the **WORLD** did them! Imagine if we were **ALL** more thoughtful of others, and more aware of the pressures those around us face. Imagine if we **ALL** tried to help out more. Imagine if everyone stopped interrupting and started using their listening switch instead. (Politicians, I'm lookin' at you!) Imagine the kind of world we could create!

Little positive actions can also make a big difference in your community. Maybe you spotted some things you could do after your Empathy Walk in **STEP 3**? It might have been deciding to pick up litter, or saying "thank you" and smiling at the key workers who do so much for our communities. Perhaps you've noticed that someone you know is lonely or having a hard time, so you've decided to be there for them. Or if you realize that someone is being bullied, you might decide to stick up for them and tell a trusted grown-up who can help. That's what being an empathy hero is all about!

My Empathy Resolution is... to stop rushing around and really listen to my friends.

You're moving from feeling or saying "I CARE" to saying "I AM WITH YOU."

That's powerful stuff, isn't it? A little shift. A **BIG** change.

EVERY HUMAN HAS A STORY

You know what's WILD when you start to really think about it? Lots of things, like the fact that lemons float but limes sink, cows moo in different accents and there's enough gold in the Earth's core to coat the entire planet in a nice, thick layer of the shiny stuff... But ALSO! The fact that every single person you pass when you're heading down a street or along a corridor is a unique human with a whole story of their own. And no two people's stories are the same. Can you imagine? They have a whole HISTORY. There is so much you don't know about them. So much you might have in common, and so much you could learn from each other.

Keeping that in mind is always useful. It'll remind you to use your empathy superpower to better understand others, and try to get an idea of WHY they feel, say or do the things they do. You'll remember not to decide what you think about others before you've really got to know and understand them.

As you now know, empathy is a skill that requires feeling AND thinking. You might find it pretty easy to feel with or understand your best friend, but a bit harder with the person who packs your groceries at the supermarket or a child who is new to your community. Or someone who has been mean to you or someone you really disagree with! You have to THINK a bit more but it IS possible to understand them better. And again, it doesn't mean you can't call it out when someone is being mean. Empathy means you understand where all of that is really coming from.

DO GOOD, FEEL GOOD, CHANGE THE WORLD!

Real empathy heroes don't do good things just because they want to be nice or charitable. They don't do it to get a sticker or a trophy or to feel smug about being kind.

An empathy hero takes time to really **UNDERSTAND** the big issues affecting our world and all the people and animals in it. They feel **INSPIRED** to help. That's why they do good things.

My Empathy Resolution is... to pick up litter so animals in the sea and in the woods don't get tangled up in it or try to eat it.

And making a difference **FEELS** good. It stirs up happy hormones like dopamine. Try it! Next time you help out at home or smile at someone you pass in the street, notice that feeling inside. Notice how doing good makes you *happy*.

It's **EMPOWERING** too. It helps you to feel as though you can actually **DO** something, which means a lot in a world where the challenges can seem so big that many of us often feel *helpless*. Instead of just worrying or feeling down about things, you can take action. And, when you do your little bit to make a positive change, you won't just feel good – you'll also feel useful and stronger.

Our Empathy Resolution is... to help people in the community by creating "Take-What-You-Need trollies" containing things like fruits and vegetables, soaps and creams for each classroom and the school reception. Students and families can take what they need, when they need it. No questions asked.

When I say "little bit" there, I really mean it. You don't have to change the world on your own. We can do it together, one teeny-tiny change at a time. All those little changes will add up to something **BIG**...

109

FIGHTING FOR WHAT'S FAIR

Empathy heroes believe in **FAIRNESS** and in **EQUALITY** – the idea that there are some things **ALL** of us deserve to have. Things like food, water, a safe place to call home. Things like the opportunity to learn stuff and grow and do well enough in life to get by *and* have money left over for some nice things.

We all deserve to be treated fairly and kindly, no matter who we are, how we look, where we're from, how our bodies or minds work or who we love. We all deserve to feel safe, cared for and as though we **BELONG**. To know we're accepted, included, **PART** of something. I mean that's just **BASIC**, right? Sadly, this isn't always the case.

But that's where empathy heroes come in! When you're an empathy hero, you **CARE**, but you also ask, **"WHAT CAN I DO TO HELP?** What would **REALLY** help?" The answer might be collecting clothes or toys or soaps and shampoos for a charity that gives them to people who need them. It might be helping to fundraise for a food bank. It might be doing what you can to raise awareness about the importance of equality and fairness, and sticking up for the rights of others. It might be speaking out when you notice that another person or group of people is being judged or treated unfairly.

When you understand that any one of us can end up in a difficult situation, you don't just feel sorry for those experiencing hardship. (We talked about this back in **STEP 1**, remember? Empathy is different from sympathy!) You're an **EMPATHY HERO**, so that means you don't feel that *distance* between you. You want to show that you're *with them*. Right by their side. You become more **DETERMINED** than ever to do what you can to make a difference.

You know that everyone has the potential to be an empathy hero too, because you truly believe that every single human is amazing and deserving of kindness and respect. But you also understand that sometimes stuff gets in the way to make things really hard for some of us – and you know that's because, sadly, this world of ours isn't very fair.

So you are going to do what **YOU** can to make it a fairer place. And I believe in you!

LEARN AND GROW

When it comes to using your empathy superpower to feel with people who are super far away or who seem incredibly different from you, there's a very handy bit of kit that will help you to imagine what they're going through.
Can you think of what it might be?

I'll give you a clue: it begins with a B.

Yep! You got it! **BOOKS**.

As you already know, reading gives you a chance to experience new worlds. And it's a powerful experience! You can drop **RIGHT** into a story (real or made-up) and feel *with* the characters, imagining what it's like to share their dreams and frustrations and challenges. Your brilliant brain **TRANSPORTS** you into someone else's life so well that it can feel as if you are actually there, experiencing a bit of what the characters experience. And when that happens, it changes you. Have you noticed that? You think about the world differently.

In fact, studies show that people who really get into a story and express empathy for the characters are more likely to be helpful towards those same groups of people afterwards. You can see how, right? If you read a book about a character who is treated terribly because of the colour of their skin or because they're disabled or because they don't have much money, you'll feel like sticking up for anyone else you notice in that situation - even if it isn't something that you have ever experienced yourself. And, if you spot someone being treated unkindly - even as a joke - you'll feel like speaking up. You'll want to show that person they're not alone, and you might even reach out to a trusted adult for help.

Another great thing about books is that they shine a light on your **OWN** behaviour. For example, you might read about one character deliberately ignoring another and think, **"WOAHHH!** They were a bit mean there... but, actually, I can be like that sometimes... **HOLD ON A SECOND!!!!** I can be better than that!"

Yep, it happens!

And just like that, you remind yourself to always use your empathy superpower. In true and made-up stories alike, you'll also find some amazing examples of empathy heroes making a difference in the world and in the lives of those around them. You can look at how *they* handle situations and the kinds of things *they* say and do, then take a leaf out of *their* book!

EMPATHY-BOOSTING ACTIVITIES

MAKE AN EMPATHY RESOLUTION

There were lots of Empathy Resolutions sprinkled throughout this chapter. Now it's your turn to make one! All you need is your amazing empathy superpower, a piece of a paper and something to write and draw with.

> My Empathy Resolution is to... really think about and understand how HUMANS feel (and not just how they taste!).

What you're going to do is come up with a promise to turn **EMPATHY** into **ACTION**. A commitment to doing something (or **NOT** doing something!) that will make a difference for other people, for our planet or for the creatures we share this world with. That's your *Empathy Resolution*.

> My Empathy Resolution is... to raise awareness about the problems young people face at home and at school.

It could be something tiny, such as Rahul's resolution to listen without interrupting. It could be something to do with your community, or it might be a big issue you really care about. Whatever it is, **WRITE IT OUT** in nice, big writing. Start with, "MY EMPATHY RESOLUTION IS..."

Now, keep your Empathy Resolution somewhere you'll see it often. This resolution is a promise, remember? **A PINKY PROMISE** with **YOURSELF**. So it's important that you don't forget it, and that you stick with it!

And hey, look, if you *do* forget sometimes, or if you find that you've messed up and haven't quite stuck with it, **THAT'S OK**. It's a learning process. If you still believe in your resolution, you can keep working at it.

Another thing you might find is that you have a shiny **LIGHT-BULB** moment and think of a way to make your resolution **EVEN BETTER**. That's OK too! It's always good to check in on your Empathy Resolution every now and then, in case there are ways you might improve it.

So have a go and make one. Then do your best to stick with it! Encourage the people around you to make one too, and see how you all get on!

And every year, EmpathyLab celebrates a **VERY** important day called **EMPATHY DAY**. It's a great chance to share your resolution with the whole world.

It might create a **WAVE** of empathy, and a **GREAT BIG WAVE** of empathy heroes!

IMAGINE the difference we could all make together!

WELLLLLLL... would
you look at that?

YOU DID IT!

You've completed
ALL SIX STEPS.

Your empathy superpower is

OFF THE CHARTS!!!!!!!

If I could, I'd get the music started and pull out a disco ball. And I'd splash it all over the news. Because **YOU DID IT!!!!!!**

Wow. We've been on quite a journey, haven't we? But it's not over just yet. I'm going to ask you to turn the page one *last time* for a final note...

You've come so far. We've come so far together.

Now you know what empathy **IS** (and what it isn't!). You know it's about moving from always thinking "Me, me, me!" to thinking about other people. You know it's about feeling what other people feel, and understanding their emotions and points of view. You know it's about connecting with others and being there for them.

You know exactly how empathy **WORKS** and what's going on inside your fantastic **PLASTIC** brain when you use empathy. Speaking of that fantastic plastic brain, you also know it's what makes empathy a learnable, **BOOSTABLE** skill. It's a **LIFE SKILL,** which you can choose to use and work on. It affects every single part of your life, and can be an **INCREDIBLE** force for change in the world.

You know empathy is a muscle that gets stronger the more you use it. **AND YOU SURE KNOW HOW TO USE IT!** You can take it out into the wild with an Empathy Walk and turn it into action with your Empathy Resolutions. You can also boost it by reading and talking about **BOOKS** and **CHARACTERS** (real or made-up), and by exploring whole new worlds inside stories. This is **SAFE MODE**. It's basically virtual reality epicness playing out inside your actual **BRAIN**. It gives you the power to really understand people who are very different from you and situations you have never experienced before. And it supercharges your empathy and **INSPIRES** you to do some good in the world.

You're **ALL OVER** emotions and feelings. You've started to grow an amazing emotional vocabulary. You can spot and understand emotions and feelings in yourself **AND** in the people around you. You've got all the tools you need to be a pro-level listener and a brilliant communicator, **WHICH,** as you know, is at the heart of being an empathy hero. And that is exactly what you are:

AN EMPATHY HERO.

You're not all style and no substance. All chat and no action. Nope. Not you. You've got that **ATTITUDE** of empathy. And you use that empathy superpower every single day to make a difference in the world, however big or small. You also know that the small stuff – such as being helpful to people around you or truly listening to others – is actually **BIG** stuff. If we all did it, we could **LITERALLY** change the world.

And that is the most incredible thing about empathy. It is our **MAP** to a kinder, better world where everyone belongs, everyone feels cared for and everyone feels safe. A map to a world where we truly care for, protect and stick up for this incredible home planet of ours, and for every person and creature and living thing we share it with.

You've already got that map. You know it works. You know where it leads. And you can share it with others!

You've done so much (and hopefully learned some interesting things along the way), but do you know something? This is only the beginning! The real adventure starts now.

Here you are, an awesome empathy hero with your shiny empathy superpower. Now it's up to **YOU** to decide what you're going to do with it...

And remember, you don't have to do it alone. We can make a difference *together*. **WE'VE GOT THIS!**

A GUIDE FOR GROWN-UPS

Empathy is an amazing life skill that affects all our relationships, our wellbeing and our chances of success in life. No matter where we are in the world, our schools and communities are incredibly diverse in every kind of way. Children need to be able to relate to others who might be different from them. They need to be able to connect and collaborate – something that their future employers will look for and value. Using empathy to understand customers' feelings and perspectives is an essential business skill too.

More importantly, empathy is a powerful force for change and a blazing beacon of hope in an increasingly divided world. It breaks down barriers and brings people closer together. It allows us to truly understand the needs of others, of our planet and of life on our planet.

Empathy has never been more important. Many people are concerned that young people today are growing up in a world with a major empathy deficit. Hate crimes are on the rise and there are increasing concerns about the negative effects of social media. An inability to extend empathy across time and space means that we're failing to tackle urgent global challenges such as climate change, war, poverty, inequality and discrimination.

But good work is happening everywhere. Throughout history and across the world, wherever we have seen a huge empathy deficit, we have also seen incredible bursts of empathy, along with the kindness and activism that empathy inspires. This book has been put together to empower children to be part of and drive that empathy movement. It's something which, at a personal level, sets them up for life, and in a wider sense also has the potential to create a far bigger wave of positive change.

Research shows that empathy is a learnable skill, which we can work on and strengthen. One of the ways we can do that is through books. There is significant scientific evidence to support the power of reading when it comes to building real-life empathy skills. Scans of readers' brains show that, as we read, our mirror neurons are activated – these brain cells fire off not just when we perform an action, but also when we observe someone else performing that action. The same applies to the feelings and sensory descriptions we encounter in books. As readers, we experience all of these things to some level alongside the characters. This is why Professor Keith Oatley from the University of Toronto calls reading "the mind's flight simulator". Like all simulations, it provides a safe environment to explore important issues and navigate tricky relationships. Through reading, we learn and grow and translate our empathy for characters in a book into empathy for people in the real world.

This book is therefore full of activities relating to books, including guidance around exploring the feelings, thoughts and actions of characters or real people in books. Use these activities as a launchpad, and help to further the discussion by asking open questions, such as those suggested in each activity. Use "I wonder" as a tool to help children to wonder about characters and their experiences. For instance, say, "I wonder what this character was feeling?" or "I wonder what it'd be like to be that character?"

"I WONDER WHAT THIS CHARACTER WAS FEELING?"

Books are also a fantastic way for children to explore issues such as injustice and inequality, racism, war and homelessness, and to connect and engage with these issues even if they don't have any personal experience of them. Compelling stories, whether real or fictional, can be life-changing. They can be immersive. Absorbing. They can widen a child's world view, open up their heart and challenge them to consider new perspectives. And importantly, stories offer children powerful role models (and anti-role models!), inspiring them to take action to make a difference in the real world.

"I WONDER WHAT IT'D BE LIKE TO BE THAT CHARACTER?"

When talking with children, listen 100 per cent to what they tell you, tuning right in. Then reflect their thoughts back to them. Help them to expand their emotional vocabulary by encouraging them to both learn and use a wide range of words to describe how they and the characters in books might be feeling. Studies show that developing a rich emotional vocabulary can work wonders for self-regulation, helping children to become aware of, explore and manage overwhelming emotions. It also strengthens their ability to recognize emotions in others.

This book is written with children in mind but I hope that even grown-ups might learn something new within these pages. I know I've learned a lot while writing this book. I know empathy is a muscle I can work harder each and every day, and I'd love it if you could join me in that endeavour. As for younger readers, you can support them in building their empathy superpower by helping them to discuss books and stories of all kinds, and encouraging them to think about the Empathy Resolutions they might be inspired to make afterwards. These resolutions are how we turn empathy into action. As a society, taking action is how we move from caring to solidarity, from instances of kindness to creating meaningful and lasting change. It's how we build a better, brighter future.

All this is to say: **EMPATHY MATTERS**.

It's learnable. It's a life skill and a force for change in the world.

And if there's one gift we can give to children – one thing that has the power to change everything – it's this.

FURTHER RESOURCES

EmpathyLab (www.empathylab.uk) has a range of powerful resources helping you use books to build empathy understanding and skills:

⭐ Help with finding empathy-rich books: annual Read for Empathy collections for 3-16 year olds (www.empathylab.uk/RFE).

⭐ Empathy Day every June: fun, creative and free resources to help children understand more about empathy (www.empathylab.uk/empathy-day).

⭐ Inspirational free resources from leading children's authors: 500-word empathy-rich stories (www.empathylab.uk/empathy-shorts).

⭐ Support for schools: resources and training to integrate an empathy focus into classrooms (www.empathylab.uk/schools-programme).

⭐ Regular newsletters: subscribe here (www.empathylab.uk).

A MESSAGE FROM EMPATHYLAB

EMPATHY BUILDERS

The Quarto Group, this book's publisher, is part of a membership scheme called Empathy Builders. This was created by EmpathyLab to celebrate and develop publishers' important role in building empathy in society. The member publishers help EmpathyLab build Empathy Day into a major force for change, aiming to involve one million children a year over the next few years.

We would like to thank every single Empathy Builder publisher
for their visionary involvement and support.

For more information visit: www.empathylab.uk/empathy-builders

THANK YOU

We would like to thank the authors, including those who have been Children's Laureates, who have allowed us to use their quotes in the book and who have contributed so generously to our work over the years: Sir Michael Morpurgo, Cressida Cowell, Joseph Coelho, Nadia Shireen, Malorie Blackman, Jacqueline Wilson, Sue Cheung, Jen Carney, Manon Steffan Ros, Ben Davis, Patrice Lawrence, Abigail Balfe; Dom Conlon and SF Said.

Thank you too to people who gave us expert help with the book: Professor Robin Banerjee, Jo Cotterill, Dr Helen Demetriou, Anne McNeil. We owe special and profound thanks to Rashmi Sirdeshpande for everything she has done to make this book possible.